ARCTIC
EXPEDITION

Written by Mike Salisbury
Illustrated by Paul Johnson

Contents

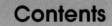

GALLERY BOOKS

ARCTIC CIRCLE PROFILE

The Arctic is a region of land and sea surrounding the North Pole, the most northerly point on earth. The Arctic Circle is an imaginary line round the Pole at a latitude of 66° North. In the center of the Circle is the Arctic Ocean, which is partly covered by a huge sheet of floating ice.

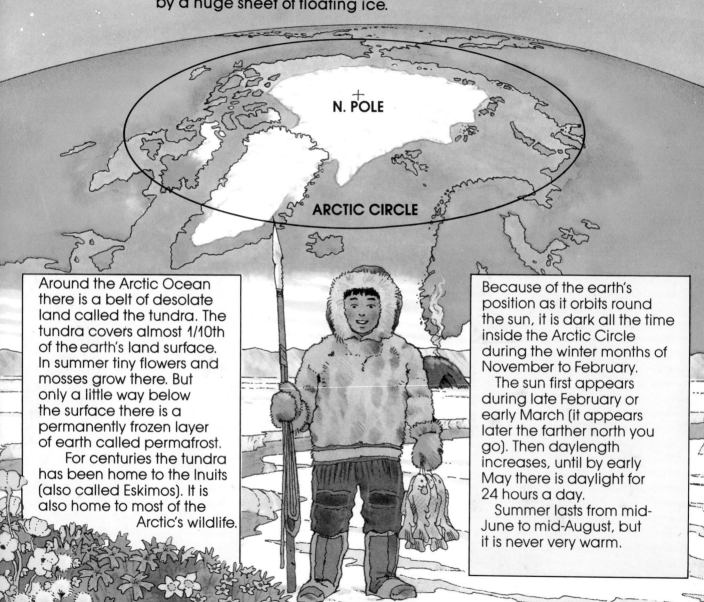

N. POLE

ARCTIC CIRCLE

Around the Arctic Ocean there is a belt of desolate land called the tundra. The tundra covers almost 1/10th of the earth's land surface. In summer tiny flowers and mosses grow there. But only a little way below the surface there is a permanently frozen layer of earth called permafrost.

For centuries the tundra has been home to the Inuits (also called Eskimos). It is also home to most of the Arctic's wildlife.

Because of the earth's position as it orbits round the sun, it is dark all the time inside the Arctic Circle during the winter months of November to February.

The sun first appears during late February or early March (it appears later the farther north you go). Then daylength increases, until by early May there is daylight for 24 hours a day.

Summer lasts from mid-June to mid-August, but it is never very warm.

Around the edge of the tundra there is a "tree line," where the earth's northern forests end. Beyond the line it is too cold for most trees to survive (the average temperature goes no higher than 50°F, even in warmest summer). The tree line can be said to be the true boundary of the Arctic region.

In winter the tundra is cold and icy. Fierce winds blow the snow into drifts, exposing patches of land here and there.

In summer the top layer of tundra ground thaws out, but the melted snow cannot drain away through the permafrost and much of the tundra becomes dotted with shallow lakes and ponds.

Arctic plants only have a two-month summer to reproduce, but when they *do* flower the barren tundra is transformed into a colorful scene.

The plants grow close to the ground as protection against the cold and wind. The temperature in this low-lying carpet of foliage can be up to 35°F warmer than the surrounding air, making it a good place for insects to live.

On areas of dry land you might see dwarf saxifrages, lupins, heathers and poppies. Most of these have hairy leaves and stems, which help to keep them warm.

The only tundra trees are the Arctic willows. Unlike most trees they grow in a flat circle. Their growth is so slow that it takes a willow about 200 years to spread only 3 ft. wide!

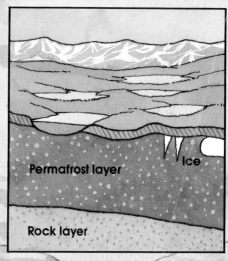

Permafrost layer

Ice

Rock layer

FIRST EXPLORERS

Lots of Arctic areas are named after the brave, early explorers who had many amazing and dangerous adventures.

The first European to reach the Arctic region was the Greek explorer Pytheas, in 325 B.C. Historians think he reached Iceland, but on his return nobody believed him, until some Irish monks rediscovered Iceland in about 750 A.D. Soon bands of Vikings arrived, and settled farther north in Greenland. There they made contact with the Inuits.

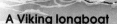

A Viking longboat

Henry Hudson cast adrift.

Between 1500 and 1900 many explorers tried to find the Northwest Passage, the sea route from Europe to China via the Arctic Ocean. When the sixteenth-century Englishman Sir Martin Frobisher reached the Arctic, he was convinced that he had actually reached China and that the Inuit people were Chinese. Frobisher Bay is named after him.

In 1610 the Englishman Henry Hudson sailed into the vast Arctic bay now named after him. He thought he had found the Northwest Passage and wanted to continue, despite terrible storms and shifting pack ice. But his crew mutinied and cast him adrift with his son.

In 1845 two British Navy ships, under the command of Sir John Franklin, disappeared while searching for the Northwest Passage.

Lady Franklin commissioned a search which revealed a few bodies and a parchment stating that the ships had been abandoned; but to this day the bodies of Sir John Franklin and most of his crew have not been found.

It was not until 1906 that Norwegian explorer Roald Amundsen finally found a way through the Arctic Ocean to the Pacific, with a twelve-man crew and a tiny ship called the *Gjoa*.

The search for Franklin.

Ross meets an Inuit.

In 1828 Sir John Ross and his cousin James Clarke Ross set out to find the Northwest Passage; but their ship got stuck in the ice for three winters. They befriended the Inuit people, and during this time James Clarke Ross mapped many Arctic Islands and found the magnetic North Pole, the only place in the world where a compass points due north (a point different from the true North Pole).

Eventually the ship was crushed in the ice, but after many difficulties and adventures the crew was finally rescued.

Many Arctic explorers have set out to reach the North Pole. In 1893 Norwegian scientist Fridtjof Nansen set off for the Arctic Ocean. In September the sea froze around his ship, the *Fram*, but because of its carefully designed round hull the ship lifted up on to the ice surface, instead of being crushed.

The *Fram* drifted slowly with the ice nearer to the North Pole. Then Nansen and a companion set out to reach the Pole on foot. They eventually got to within 269 mi. of their goal — nearer than any previous human. On their return journey they nearly starved, but were finally rescued in May 1896.

The *Fram*

The *Nautilus*

It was not until 1909 that a human being first stood at the North Pole. The man who achieved this remarkable feat was the American explorer Robert Peary.

In 1959 the U.S. Navy's atomic submarine *Nautilus* heralded a new type of Arctic travel, when it became the first submarine to cross the Arctic underneath the ice.

Nowadays, you can fly to the Arctic, land near the Pole, and be back in the warmth of a northern weather station, all within 24 hours!

ARCTIC EQUIPMENT

It is important to take the right equipment on an Arctic trip. Some of the items you will need are shown below.

You must not skimp on Arctic clothing because it will keep you warm enough to survive! You could either get a set of Inuit clothes made from animal skin (see p.25), or take with you the clothes shown below. Either way you should wear as many layers as you can, because this creates warm air pockets around your body.

Bright Arctic sunlight reflects strongly off white snow and ice. This can cause people to suffer from snow blindness, a painful feeling as if your eyes are full of very sharp dust! Good quality dark glasses will cut out the harmful light rays.

INSIDE LAYERS   OUTER LAYERS

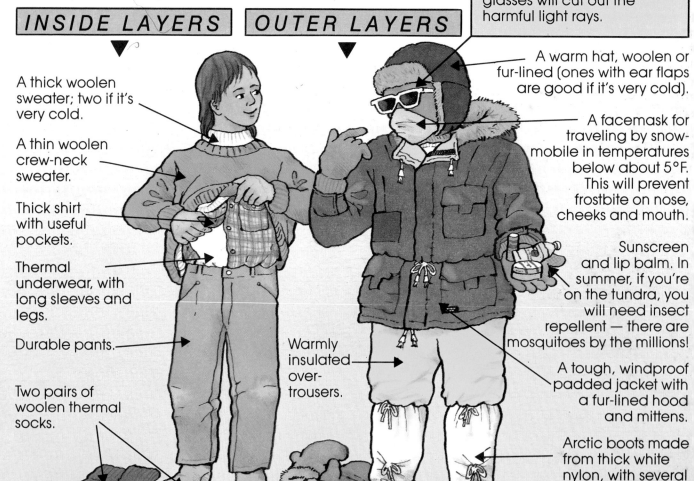

A thick woolen sweater; two if it's very cold.

A thin woolen crew-neck sweater.

Thick shirt with useful pockets.

Thermal underwear, with long sleeves and legs.

Durable pants.

Two pairs of woolen thermal socks.

Warmly insulated over-trousers.

A warm hat, woolen or fur-lined (ones with ear flaps are good if it's very cold).

A facemask for traveling by snow-mobile in temperatures below about 5°F. This will prevent frostbite on nose, cheeks and mouth.

Sunscreen and lip balm. In summer, if you're on the tundra, you will need insect repellent — there are mosquitoes by the millions!

A tough, windproof padded jacket with a fur-lined hood and mittens.

Arctic boots made from thick white nylon, with several layers of insulating material inside.

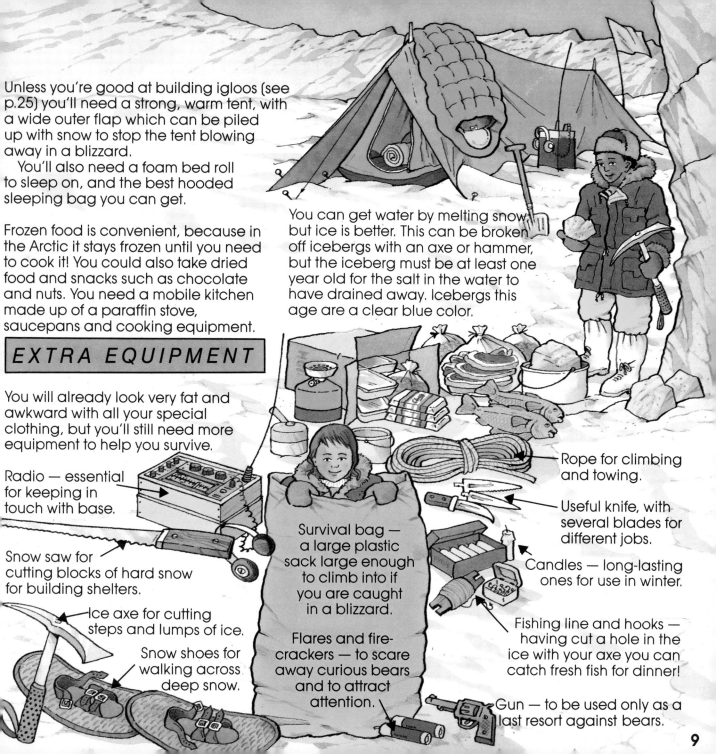

Unless you're good at building igloos (see p.25) you'll need a strong, warm tent, with a wide outer flap which can be piled up with snow to stop the tent blowing away in a blizzard.

You'll also need a foam bed roll to sleep on, and the best hooded sleeping bag you can get.

Frozen food is convenient, because in the Arctic it stays frozen until you need to cook it! You could also take dried food and snacks such as chocolate and nuts. You need a mobile kitchen made up of a paraffin stove, saucepans and cooking equipment.

EXTRA EQUIPMENT

You will already look very fat and awkward with all your special clothing, but you'll still need more equipment to help you survive.

Radio — essential for keeping in touch with base.

Snow saw for cutting blocks of hard snow for building shelters.

Ice axe for cutting steps and lumps of ice.

Snow shoes for walking across deep snow.

You can get water by melting snow, but ice is better. This can be broken off icebergs with an axe or hammer, but the iceberg must be at least one year old for the salt in the water to have drained away. Icebergs this age are a clear blue color.

Rope for climbing and towing.

Useful knife, with several blades for different jobs.

Survival bag — a large plastic sack large enough to climb into if you are caught in a blizzard.

Flares and fire-crackers — to scare away curious bears and to attract attention.

Candles — long-lasting ones for use in winter.

Fishing line and hooks — having cut a hole in the ice with your axe you can catch fresh fish for dinner!

Gun — to be used only as a last resort against bears.

Arctic travel is difficult and dangerous. Without careful planning a trip could end in disaster.

Husky dog teams and wooden sleds used to be the only method of Arctic winter travel.

Nowadays snowmobiles are more often used. They are similar to motorcycles, but have skis at the front and a ribbed belt at the back.

Walking was once the only way to cross the land in summer, but now you can use an A.T.V. (All Terrain Vehicle), a motorized tricycle with three balloon tires which help absorb bumps and stop the A.T.V. sinking in boggy ground.

To get to the farthest corners of the Arctic it is best to travel by airplane or helicopter. The most popular aircraft is the De Havilland Twin Otter, which can

land or take off in distances as short as 600 ft., and can be fitted with skis or balloon tires.

Helicopters can land on very small patches of ground or even on drifting ice-floes. However, they use a lot of fuel, so for long journeys you would need to organize fuel stores along your route.

Journeys over Arctic pack ice can be dangerous, because storms or tides can cause large areas of sea ice to break up and start moving. If you see cracks widening, you must race to a firmer area.

A change of wind or tide can bring ice floes together, crushing all but the strongest ships. Only icebreakers with reinforced hulls can make headway through the ice.

A.T.V.

Snowmobile

Expedition difficulties are often due to isolation from human help. The average distance from the tree line to the North Pole is 1426 mi., and in all that distance you might meet only a handful of people!

Radio contact is very important. In the Canadian Arctic, explorers must report to a base station twice a day, at 7 a.m. and 7 p.m.

If you miss three of your radio calls, a rescue plane will be sent to look for you, but if you have simply forgotten to call in, you will have to pay the cost of the search!

Inuit families have their own radio frequencies to contact each other. It is difficult to have a private radio conversation, because there are often lots of other people listening in.

Blowing snow sometimes causes "whiteouts," which can start suddenly and last for days. In these conditions it is impossible to see anything.

If you get caught in a difficult place, such as on a glacier, it is better to stop and camp until the white out is over. This is a good reason for always carrying your tent, sleeping bag and rations with you.

Arctic survival depends on keeping warm. The greatest danger is windchill — when a strong wind brings the temperature down to dangerous levels. At −31°F bare flesh freezes within 1 minute, so if the wind gets bitingly fierce you must find shelter, by digging a hole in the snow if necessary.

Two major dangers are frostbite and hypothermia, which begins with shivering and drowsiness and should be quickly prevented with hot drinks and a warm sleeping bag. Frostbite starts on the hands, feet and face; first the skin goes white and then all feeling is lost. The best cure is to gently warm the affected area, for instance by putting your feet on someone's warm stomach.

11

LARGE TUNDRA ANIMALS

Most Arctic animals live on the tundra only during the summer months, finding shelter in the forests or underground during winter. Some of the largest tundra creatures are shown below.

Grizzly bears hibernate in dens during winter, so you would only see one between March and late October.

An adult male can weigh up to 790 lbs. One record animal weighed a massive 1500 lbs.

Grizzlies eat grass, fungi, berries, insects, small mammals, fish and sometimes caribou. They might even visit your camp if they can smell food cooking!

A grizzly will growl and lay its ears back if it wants to attack. If this happens you must back away slowly and calmly. Hopefully, the bear will then lose interest.

The most common large Arctic animal is the tundra deer, called the caribou in North America and the reindeer in Europe.

In Scandinavia reindeer are kept in herds by the Lapp people. In Canada and Alaska, the caribou roam free, gathering into vast herds to travel from their winter home in the forests to their summer home on the tundra.
A moving herd is an amazing wildlife spectacle, sometimes numbering over a hundred thousand animals.

▼

Grizzly bear

Wolverine

◀ The wolverine is one of the rarest animals in the tundra, seen only in remote areas. An adult can grow up to about 3 ft. long.

To keep warm, wolverines have two sets of fur: a thick, soft underfur with larger "guard" hairs forming an outer layer.

Wolverines are solitary creatures; they range over large territories, which they mark out with a distinctive musk odor. They eat small mammals, baby caribou and carrion, and they also eat berries when they can find them.

Musk oxen
defend their herd.

Musk oxen stay on the tundra all year long. They have large curved horns and are covered in an outer coat of dense, long hair. Underneath there is a layer of fine wool, which they shed each May when the weather gets warmer. Small birds often gather the discarded fleece from rocks and bushes, to make cozy nests.

Musk oxen herds are peaceful, but if a predator such as a wolf or a bear appears, the adults form a defensive ring facing outwards and one of the bulls will charge to scare off the enemy. During August the oxen mate, and the strongest male tries to chase off his rivals. The oxen charge at each other and sometimes crash head-on at up to 31 mph.

Arctic wolf

Wolves can often be seen following herds of caribou. Their fur ranges in color from almost black to pure white. They live in packs, hunting together by chasing their prey into an ambush or running in relays to keep a herd in turmoil until a weak animal can be picked off.

Sometimes wolves howl together, in an eerie chorus which biologists think may help to keep a pack together. The noise can often be heard up to 10 mi. away. Wolves have been feared and hunted for centuries, but attacks on humans are actually very rare.

SMALL TUNDRA ANIMALS

There are many small animals on the tundra throughout the year. Some of them stay above the surface in winter, and some hide in burrows under the hard crust of snow.

There are several species of Arctic lemmings, small rodents which live in underground burrows during winter, feeding on buried plant shoots.

The lemmings begin to breed in spring. Each female can produce five or six young at a time and have up to five litters each season.

Numbers increase very quickly, causing population explosions every four years or so. Then some animals have to migrate to new feeding areas, to avoid starvation. Many die of exhaustion and lack of food on the journey, or drown trying to swim across stretches of water. The lemming population is cut down, and then the four-year cycle starts again.

▼

Ermine

Many animals rely on lemmings for food. For instance, weasels and ermine are small enough to chase lemmings down their burrows.

Ermine fur turns white in winter, when it is prized by human hunters.

Arctic ground squirrels build elaborate tunnel systems underground. Many different species of animals use these tunnels to hibernate from November to March.

Ground squirrel

Weasel

Collared lemmings

The white Arctic hares are the largest hares in the World, weighing up to 15 lbs. When the icy wind blows strongly, they will sit for hours with their ears back and their legs tucked under their body. Huddled like this only their fur-covered paws touch the snow.

Arctic fox

Arctic hare

Arctic foxes are pure white in winter, but in summer their fur turns a spotted brown. In some areas they feed mainly on lemmings, and they adjust the number of cubs that are born each spring according to the lemming population — the more lemmings the larger the litter.

Foxes are always on the lookout for food, and will eat eggs, birds, berries and small animals. In winter they follow polar bears far out onto the sea ice to feed on leftover pieces of food. They will often turn up at camps looking for scraps. They have a trusting nature and little fear of humans; but many thousands are trapped and killed for their fur every year.

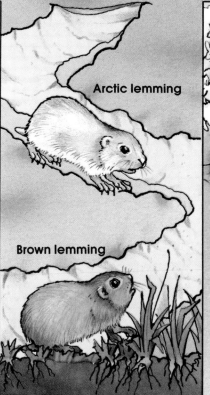

Arctic lemming

Brown lemming

Arctic hares mate in April and May, after "boxing" matches and extraordinary running and leaping displays by the males.

Some Arctic hares herd together. Hundreds, even thousands, of the animals gather, feeding or running in a tightly bunched mass that can be easily mistaken for a mysteriously flowing patch of snow!

ARCTIC BIRDS

Over 100 different species of bird breed in the Arctic, but most of these are summer visitors. Very few species are adapted to survive the extreme cold, the darkness and the shortage of food in winter.

WINTER BIRDS

Ptarmigan have speckled brown plumage in summer and white plumage in winter. It even grows on their legs and feet. In very cold weather they sometimes burrow under the snow for warmth and to find willow shoots or old berries.

Snowy owl

Ptarmigan

The brilliant white snowy owl makes an unforgettable winter sight, staring with piercing eyes or swooping silently down to snatch food.

The owl survives the winter by eating any dead creatures it finds or any lemmings foolish enough to come to the surface.

During winter you may hear a raven's croak. Ravens and Arctic redpolls spend winter near the tundra tree line.

Raven

Redpoll

SUMMER BIRDS

The Arctic summer lasts for barely two months, so birds visiting from the south must arrive as soon as the snow begins to clear in late May. They raise their young as quickly as possible and fly south again before the end of August, when harsh winter weather returns to the tundra.

Lots of geese arrive in May, flying in spectacular V-shaped formations. Common ones include the brent, white-fronted, pink-footed, greater and lesser snow and barnacle geese.

To avoid predators, especially Arctic foxes (who don't like swimming), the geese often nest on small islands or take their goslings to tundra lakes as soon as possible.

In Arctic Greenland, barnacle geese nest high up on rocky ledges, where there is no grass to eat. The young goslings must make the journey down to find food and, encouraged by their parents, they jump over the ledge. They cannot fly, so they float down and bounce on the rocks below. Only half of them survive the fall.

In summer over 30 types of waders and several diving birds come to feed in the tundra lakes and ponds. One example is the red-throated diver bird, which can stay underwater for up to three minutes.

Widgeon

Teal

Old squaw

Phalarope

Plover

Turnstone

Eider duck

Many species of duck nest near the tundra lakes, where they dabble in the water for food. Examples include widgeon, teal and pintails.

At deeper lakes you will see diving ducks such as old squaw and mergansers. You may also see common and king eider ducks.

The mother eider duck lines her nest with very soft "down" from her breast. This material is one of the world's best natural insulators, which means that it stops heat from escaping through it. It is often collected by people to fill bedding and line clothes.

Arctic birds of prey include buzzards, peregrines, and gyr falcons. The falcons feed on small birds, which they catch in midair after panicking them to leave their nests.

Lots of small insect-eating birds, such as larks, wheatears and pipits, arrive in summer. Snow bunting are the first to appear in May: their song brings the tundra alive after the long winter.

Gyr falcon

Snow bunting

SEABIRDS

Millions of seabirds migrate northwards each summer to breed in the Arctic. They take advantage of the plentiful food supply uncovered when the ice breaks up. Some common species are shown below.

Fulmars are graceful, gliding flyers with narrow wings. They catch small fish and crustaceans in the open patches of water between ice floes.

The fulmars nest on high cliff edges from May onwards. Their traditional nesting sites become very crowded, with up to 100,000 breeding pairs.

When a particularly popular fulmar breeding area is shared in even greater numbers by the other two major cliff-nesting species, Brünnich's guillemot and the kittiwake, the sight is spectacular.

On the famous cliffs of Prince Leopold Islands, in the Canadian Arctic, more than half a million seabird pairs nest in summer. This amazing site has deservedly been called one of the bird-watching wonders of the world.

Fulmar

Kittiwake

Brünnich's guillemot

Little auk

Glaucous gull

Ivory gull

Little auks are the most abundant of all the seabirds breeding in the Arctic. They nest on rocky slopes in huge colonies, and the total number of pairs visiting the Arctic each summer has been estimated to be 17½ million — that's an incredible 35 million individual birds!

Large gray glaucous gulls breed on the cliffs in smaller numbers. They prey on the other birds, patrolling nesting ledges looking for unattended eggs or chicks to feed on.

Of all the gulls you might see in the north, the most truly Arctic is the ivory gull, a beautiful creamy-white bird with black legs and a light yellow bill.
  These gulls breed in small groups on isolated rocky shorelines, feeding mostly among the pack ice. In winter they move only as far as the southern edge of the annual ice.

Arctic terns nest on shoreline tundra or shingle banks. They catch fish and plankton to feed to their chicks, who develop quickly during July and August in readiness for the longest of all known bird migrations.
  The terns leave the Arctic in September, and their journey takes them down the entire length of the Atlantic and Pacific Oceans and on into the Antarctic pack ice at the other end of the world. They then fly the return journey the following June. This breathtaking trek is a tremendous feat of endurance for such a small bird.

Arctic sea temperatures range from approx 28°F in winter to just above freezing point by the end of summer. The cold water would quickly kill humans, but Arctic animals such as seals, walruses and whales have warm layers of insulating fat called blubber.

Although the surface of the sea ice may be frozen and lifeless, the underside is very different. From March onwards sunlight filters through up to 6 ft. of ice, and a layer of greenish-brown algae grows on the ice undersurface. The simple plants form the basis of the food chain on which all Arctic sea creatures depend.

Many tiny shrimp-like creatures called amphipods "graze" upside-down on the algae. They in turn are eaten by polar and Arctic cod.

Both cod and amphipods are eaten by whales, seals and seabirds, and at the very top of the food chain there is the polar bear, which feeds mainly on seals.

Ringed seal

Bearded seal

Ringed seals stay in the Arctic all year round, living mostly under the ice and basking on the surface in summer. To survive under the ice the seals must keep a breathing hole open. Using teeth and flippers they dig out a funnel shape to the surface, with an opening to the air.

In spring a pregnant seal will make a "birth lair," a chamber next to a breathing hole where it will give birth to one pup. The lair helps to hide the family from any hungry polar bears.

Bearded seals also live under the Arctic ice all year round and keep breathing holes open in winter. Their name comes from their beard of stiff sensitive hair, which they use to feel along the seabed for food.

Bearded seal hide is very strong and waterproof and it has always been prized by the Inuit for making boots and skin-covered boats.

Walruses are famous for their ivory tusks, which can grow up to 3 ft. long on an adult male. These fat creatures can weigh up to 2200 lbs., but when they swim they become fast and graceful. They can dive to depths of about 240 ft. and hold their breath for up to 9 minutes.

Once the walruses reach the bottom they find shellfish and crush them between their teeth. Then they suck out the food from inside. They sometimes kill and eat seals, so if you are diving near them be careful — they might mistake *you* for a seal!

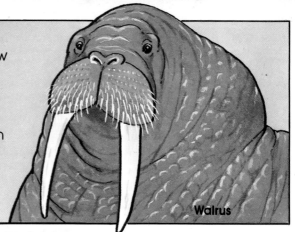

Walrus

Harp seals

Harp seals spend the winter south of the pack ice and swim north in spring, grouping together in huge numbers to breed.

The pups are born on the ice in March or April, and for the first 2–4 weeks they have pure white fur. Thousands of pups were once killed every year for their skins by Canadian hunters; but the numbers have dropped since there has been worldwide publicity on the cruelty of the seal hunt.

Three species of whale live among the Arctic pack ice. One of these is the bowhead, also known as the "right whale," because being slow and easy to catch it was once the "right" creature to hunt.

Bowheads have a curved upper jaw hung with a curtain of baleen plates. As the whales swim along, water is forced through the plates, which acting like giant sieves trap amphipods for the whale to eat.

Bowhead

Narwhal

Beluga

The other two truly Arctic whales are the beluga (or white whale) and the narwhal. Both species gather to feed on amphipods and fish at the floe edge (where the Arctic ice sheet meets the ocean). Narwhal are sometimes known as sea unicorns, because the males grow an extraordinary spiralled tusk, sometimes 9 ft. long. Adult belugas are pure white and show up beautifully in the clear Arctic waters.

POLAR BEARS

"Nanook" is the Inuit name for the polar bear, meaning "ice bear." It is the most impressive, most feared animal found roaming the Arctic, and no visit would be complete without seeing one.

   Adult male polar bears can weigh around 1320lbs. and measure 11 ft. from nose to tail. This makes them one of the largest land carnivores in the world.

Polar bears have good eyesight and very sensitive noses. As a bear wanders across the ice it will frequently point its head upwards to sniff the air, testing for the faintest smell that might lead to a seal — or a tent where explorers are cooking their breakfast! Bears have been seen detecting prey from several miles away. They can also locate ringed seal pups in birth lairs (see p. 20) under at least 3 ft. of snow. The bears use their immense weight to crash through the roof and grab their prey.

   With large teeth designed for tearing flesh and claws as sharp as a tiger's, the polar bear is a formidable hunter.

The bears roam the frozen seas all over the Arctic, looking for their main prey, the ringed seal. They can plod long distances, and run for short bursts at up to 25 mph.

   Considering their great size the bears are remarkably agile, and they can swim well, diving to depths of several feet for up to two minutes. One of the ways they catch seals unaware is to glide slowly towards one, with only their head above water. However, most seals are caught by bears crouching patiently for hours by a breathing hole.

Mating occurs from March to May. Then, during October and November, the pregnant females wander away from the sea ice into the coastal hills and valleys to find places where the shifting snow creates a drift. Here they dig their maternity dens, so that by midwinter, when they give birth to between 1 and 3 cubs, they will be totally hidden under the surface.

In March the female bears break out of their dens, and they can often be seen sliding down the slopes and rolling on their backs in what looks like sheer delight at being back outside. Since they have not eaten since November they emerge thin and hungry.

Within a few days a mother bear will take her cubs on short outings to strengthen their legs. Gradually the family will go farther.

Mothers are very attentive to their cubs, stopping to rest and suckle them every now and then; but these first weeks on the sea ice are extremely dangerous and many cubs die. Apart from getting lost and separated from their mother the greatest risk to the cubs is being killed by large male polar bears, who are also roaming the ice looking for food.

Cubs that *do* survive stay with their mother for 2½ years, learning from her and practicing various ways to catch seals, until they can manage on their own.

Polar bears will feast on berries and other vegetation in season, but they also have a fascination for *anything* they think might be edible, including expedition equipment such as tents, boots, rubber boats, snowmobile seats, engine oil and even humans!

The best way to scare a bear away is by using flares or firecrackers. If these don't work the very last resort would be to use a gun, but it is much better to keep a sharp lookout for bears and deter them before they get too close.

ARCTIC PEOPLE

The people of the Arctic were once called Eskimos. This means "eating it raw" in North American Indian language. It refers to the Eskimo habit of eating uncooked meat, and was probably originally meant as an insult. The Arctic inhabitants now prefer to be called Inuit — which in their language means "the people."

There are about 100,000 Inuit spread across Greenland, Alaska, Canada and Siberia. They speak two main languages: Yupik in Southwest Alaska and Siberia, and Inupiaq from Canadian North Alaska across to Greenland. There are many different dialects within the two languages.

For the last 20,000 years groups of Inuit have hunted animals for food and clothing. They developed a traveling way of life, settling for short periods where the hunting was good, building igloo shelters, and then moving on when the animals left.

Some Inuit continue to follow this pattern, while others have settled in one place.

Inuit knowledge has been passed on by word of mouth for centuries. They have a long tradition of storytelling; a good way of spending some of the long hours of winter darkness. Funny and courageous tales of hunting exploits are particularly popular. Especially large igloos used to be built in winter, so that groups could get together to swap news and share food.

Traditional Inuit houses vary depending on the season or area. The best known is the igloo, a dome shape built from snow blocks. Inside an igloo sleeping rugs of caribou or polar bear fur are spread out and a stone lamp is lit, which uses seal oil for fuel and cotton grass as a wick. It gives out heat as well as light.

Small igloos are occasionally still built for overnight hunting stops. Large meeting-place igloos are more luxurious, with snow benches and windows made from ice sheets. Nowadays in summer roomy canvas tents are used, but the traditional ones were made of caribou hides and driftwood tent poles.

Many Inuit now wear modern clothes, but their traditional dress is much warmer.

Caribou or bear skin jackets are made loose-fitting, so that the wearer will not get hot and uncomfortable. The hood is usually trimmed with wolf fur.

Big fur mittens, usually wolf skin, keep the hands warm.

Traditionally trousers are made from animal skin. The warmest pairs have two layers, one with fur facing the inside and one with fur facing the outside.

The best Arctic boots are made of waterproof bearded seal skin, sewn together with walrus-hide thread which swells up when wet and stops water getting in through the needle holes. Sometimes these boots have a lining of soft fur, or they are stuffed with dry grass.

The Inuit are an artistic people, and often spend many long winter hours making traditional carvings from soapstone or ivory.

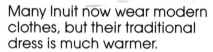

For centuries everything the Inuit needed for food and clothing had to come from animals, so they developed great hunting skills which some Inuit still use today. Small boys start to learn how to hunt at a very young age.

Many Inuit still find that their traditional hunting weapons are just as effective as modern rifles. The throwing spear has always been their main weapon. At the tip it has a detachable toothed harpoon, carved out of walrus or narwhal ivory. Attached to the harpoon is a long line which the hunter grabs to stop his prey escaping.

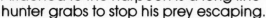

During winter seals must keep breathing holes open in the sea ice (see p.20). Dogs are used to sniff out these spots and a hunter will then make a small opening above the breathing hole. Across this he lays a thin bone with a tiny hair of down attached.

The idea is to crouch quite still, sometimes for many hours, waiting for the seal to return. As soon as the hair moves the hunter thrusts downwards with his harpoon.

Polar bears are hunted in late winter, as they wander the sea ice in the first sunlight of the year.

A hunter will follow a set of bear tracks, and when he spots his prey he will let loose two of his fastest dogs to chase it. He will quickly unload luggage to lighten his sled, and then he will chase after them. A polar bear will always head for open water, and can escape by swimming away.

Nowadays there is a limit set on the number of polar bears killed each season.

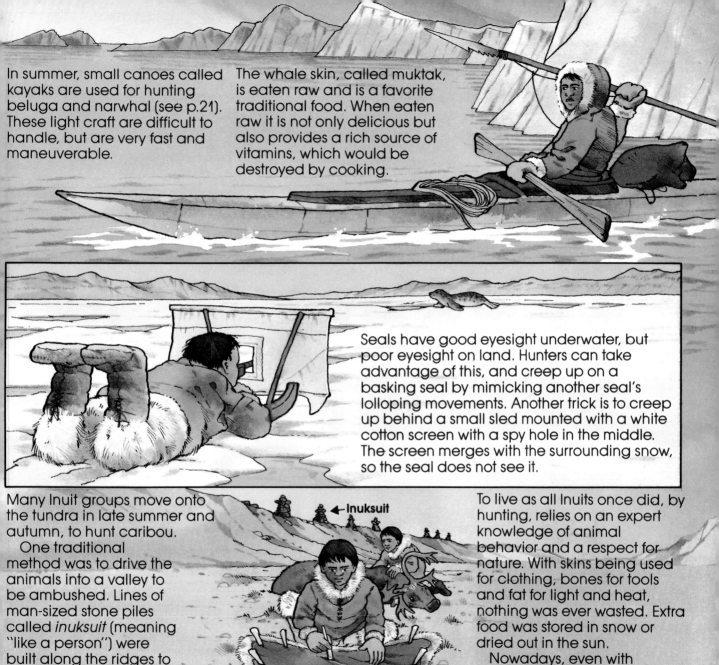

In summer, small canoes called kayaks are used for hunting beluga and narwhal (see p.21). These light craft are difficult to handle, but are very fast and maneuverable.

The whale skin, called muktak, is eaten raw and is a favorite traditional food. When eaten raw it is not only delicious but also provides a rich source of vitamins, which would be destroyed by cooking.

Seals have good eyesight underwater, but poor eyesight on land. Hunters can take advantage of this, and creep up on a basking seal by mimicking another seal's lolloping movements. Another trick is to creep up behind a small sled mounted with a white cotton screen with a spy hole in the middle. The screen merges with the surrounding snow, so the seal does not see it.

Many Inuit groups move onto the tundra in late summer and autumn, to hunt caribou.

One traditional method was to drive the animals into a valley to be ambushed. Lines of man-sized stone piles called *inuksuit* (meaning "like a person") were built along the ridges to scare the caribou and guide them towards the hunters, hidden in waiting.

← Inuksuit

To live as all Inuits once did, by hunting, relies on an expert knowledge of animal behavior and a respect for nature. With skins being used for clothing, bones for tools and fat for light and heat, nothing was ever wasted. Extra food was stored in snow or dried out in the sun.

Nowadays, even with supplies of manufactured food and clothing, many Inuit still like to go hunting to provide for their families.

27

ARCTIC UPDATE

The Arctic is the largest wilderness area left in the world, and the skills of Inuit hunters have enabled them to live there for centuries without wasting its wildlife. But the Arctic environment is now increasingly threatened by modern developments.

The Arctic has rich reserves of oil and gas, but it is very expensive to get them out. The pipelines have to be laid above ground, where they sometimes block the migrating routes of the caribou (see p.12). One answer is to raise the pipelines into bridges.

The Arctic is rich in minerals, but the movement of heavy mining equipment across the tundra leaves deep tracks in the ground. Because Arctic plant growth is so slow these scars on the land can last for fifty or more years.

To avoid this, ice roads are made, crossing frozen land and water for many hundreds of miles.

Scientists are trying to learn more about the Arctic environment, to try to limit industrial damage to plants and wildlife. Already they have discovered that some areas are being polluted by chemical waste. New expeditions can help by testing air and water for pollution.

The Inuit have the best knowledge of Arctic survival, but many are worried that their age-old culture will gradually die out as their way of life changes.

Although some Inuit groups still live traditionally, many have now moved into purpose-built settlements. They often work in the oil or mining industries, but their jobs are insecure and families often live in poverty, having forgotten their old hunting skills.

CONSERVE THE ARCTIC

With modern transport and equipment humans can now reach the farthest corners of the Arctic, so it is important that we quickly find out more about its ecology. Then the bad effects of disturbance and industrial pollution can be judged and prevented.

Some rich wildlife areas have now been declared protected reserves, and endangered animals such as the polar bear have been saved by international agreements which limit hunting.

We must learn as much as we can about the Arctic, so we can preserve its unique wildlife and exciting landscape. If you go there one day you might be able to help!

INDEX

If you would like to know more about preservation of wildlife in the Arctic you can contact the addresses shown below:

Arctic Environmental Information and Data Center
University of Alaska
707 A Street
Anchorage, AK 99501

National Geographic Society
17th and M Streets NW
Washington D.C. 20036